THE TRUE STORY OF THE SWORD IN THE STONE:

A COMPENDIUM ON THE LIFE OF ST. GALGANO

Sopraffatto, e contrito cadde Galgano al suolo, e trattasi dal fianco la spada, esclamò: come ti degni clementissimo Signore tanto favorire un miserabile peccatore! Ah che io potrò più facilmente immergere la spada in questo sasso, che ottener perdono alle mie tante colpe: spintala ciò detto, contro il medesimo, tutta vi s'immerse fino all'elsa.

THE TRUE STORY OF THE SWORD IN THE STONE

A COMPENDIUM OF THE LIFE OF ST. GALGANO

by Torchj Dei Gius Galetti

Translated from the Italian
of the 1835 Florentine edition by
Ryan Grant

Edited by Sarah Grant

MEDIATRIX PRESS
MMXIV

ISBN: 978-1-953746-36-8

Translated from:
Compendio della vita di San Galgano
1835
Firenze

Published 25 November, 2014
©Mediatrix Press. All rights reserved.
This work may not be reproduced in electronic or physical format except for reviews in journals, or classroom use without the permission of the publisher.

All images are in the public domain.

Table of Contents

Chapter I
    The First Years of Galgano........... 1

Chapter II
    His Conversion. 3

Chapter III
    He is Admonished in a Vision to Retire to
    Mount Siepi to do Penance 6

Chapter IV
    Galgano's Relatives Come to Propose him
    a Bride, and he sets off to see Her.. ... 9

Chapter V
    The Beginning of his Penance.. 13

Chapter VI
    Galgano is Found by Some Hunters that
    give news of him in Chiusdino; his Mother
    and Relatives visit him, and also bring the
    would be Bride 17

Chapter VII
    Galgano has the Divine approval to
    receive an Indulgence in Rome........ 21

Chapter VIII
> Galgano has a Revelation of what happened while in Rome, urges the Pope for the Relics, and Returns to Mount Siepi 25

Chapter IX
> The Penitential Life of Galgano and some Graces Obtained through his Intercession. 28

Chapter X
> The Death of St. Galgano............ 32

Chapter XI
> God Miraculously Provides for his Burial. 34

Chapter XII
> The Origin of the Chapel and Abbey of St. Galgano......................... 38

Chapter XIII
> Galgano is Canonized and Enrolled in the Number of Confessors, and some Miracles. 43

Chapter XIV
> Extraction of his Precious Relics, and Especially the Sacred Head........... 46

Chapter XV
> The Veneration in which the Sacred Head is always held, and the Various Miracles Granted to its Intercession .
> 52

Conclusion. 56

Epilogue
> by dom Noah Moerbeek,
> *Christi Pauperum Militiae Templi Ordo*
> 58

Translator's Preface

It is with great joy that I present for the first time in the English language, a work of any length on St. Galgano. Some of his story is already known to English speaking audiences, though through entirely other means, namely, the medieval stories of King Arthur.

The sword in the stone, though a significant miracle in St. Galgano's life, is but a divine confirmation of his calling to penance, prayer and sacrifice for souls, whereas in Arthurian legend it is centered around the establishment of an earthly kingdom. This introduction into the Arthurian legend is late, around the 14th century, and most certainly has its origin in the story of St. Galgano.

From the 18th century to the present, it was thought that the sword was a fake, a local medieval legend. This was completely shattered in 2001, when scientists from the University of Pavia, headed by Luigi Garlaschelli, conducted a study on the sword, and found that it was indeed authentic. The metallurgy was of a 12th century composition, employing no modern alloys, simply being tempered iron. The cavity in the rock outlines the blade exactly, something entirely beyond medieval technology. Even a sword composed today could not produce so exact an entrance into a boulder. This miracle should be taken as God's confirmation to Galgano of the life he was to lead, and not something deserving admiration in itself.

As to the text, it is a simple and straightforward narrative, written in 19th century Italian, mostly in the third person. It is short on details we might like to see, as, alas, it is a compendium drawn from a number of other sources. It is designed to help the reader enter into the life of St. Galgano with a spirit of prayer and admiration for the work which God was about to carry out in the soul of the saint, as well as inspire us to strive likewise in that direction.

While we would perhaps like to know more about what Galgano said on this or that occasion, or at the confrontation with his relatives on Mount Siepi, we must be satisfied with the narrative that the author has provided us, which I have striven to faithfully render out of the antiquated Italian without any nuance, except for making it more pleasing to English speech by replacing the numerous participles with finite verbs.

May the reader find inspiration from this obscure saint, to not only conquer sin, but to strive to empty himself of the love of this world, and look upon God for Whom our hearts were made, and without Whom they are restless. In the famous and beautiful words of St. Augustine of Hippo, *"Cor nostrum inquietum est, donec requiescat in te."*

    Ryan Grant
    Post Falls, ID
    22 November, 2014

Sancto Michaeli Archangelo,
custodi Ecclesiæ, ut eandem
cum ab impetibus diaboli
tum expugnationibus sæculi
nostri defendat.

Incominciò il corso del fervoroso e breve ritiro, venerando in quella spada la figura della Croce, che attesa la conformazione dell'elsa esattamente rappresentava, nè volle altra farne, onde avere sempre davanti gli occhi la misericordia infinita del Signore.

CHAPTER I
The First Years of Galgano

IN the year of our Savior, 1148, Galgano was born of Guidotto Guidotti and his wife, Dionisia, in Chiusdino which, though today is a little country, was in the times of which we write, populous and possessed of a strong castle. This was situated on a steep hill at a distance of about eighteen miles from Siena, in the direction of Massa Marittima. Little is known of Guidotto Guidotti's lineage; for the family of Guidotti was distant and ascribed to the citizens of Siena, which at that time was a very considerable republic and among the most powerful in Italy. To call this to mind is not so as to add any luster to the merits of our Galgano, as if a birthplace can be an asset increasing unto virtue, but indeed renders more despicable the vice; rather, it is only to serve the truth of history, which circumstances also show how important the castle of Chiusdino was in the Middle Ages.

THE TRUE STORY OF THE SWORD IN THE STONE

Since he was provided with an abundance of goods, Guidotto could give his son the best education that the roughness of the times allowed. He was perverted by bad examples which, unfortunately, abounded in that age, for idleness is a frequent companion of affluence, and thus Galgano abandoned himself to all the disorders of unbridled youth. His exceedingly afflicted parents, who were mannered and religious, tried every means to recall him to the right path.

Sadly, during this time, Galgano's father died, but not without remonstrating with his son and reminding him of holy things, always hoping in the infinite mercy of the Lord to bring his wayward son to conversion. The reprobate Galgano, being free from the subjection of his father, launched himself with greater impetus into the whirlwind of passion, until it pleased the Lord, with a particular stretch of His mercy, to stop him in the middle of his course and call him to the road of salvation.

THE TRUE STORY OF THE SWORD IN THE STONE

CHAPTER II
His Conversion

While away from his mother, Galgano stayed in Siena to pick a home better suited to entertainment and pleasure, with a secondary sight set upon a military career. This was very dangerous, not only as it is today, but more so in that time as it was seldom separated from violence and robbery. As it happened, however, he was favored with a striking vision, the description of which is as follows.

In the middle of the night, St. Michael the Archangel appeared. He saw also his mother, to whom St. Michael was speaking, admonishing and encouraging her to consent to the idea of her son enlisting in the heavenly militia. What honor such a gift should bring to her motherly heart. Galgano saw her bow deeply and nod her consent, then saw himself follow the footsteps of

The True Story of the Sword in the Stone

the Angel.

The young man became restless, and with a sudden resolve abandoned all his amusements, the very things that kept him in Siena. He returned to his father's house, and in a humble and affectionate manner, he told his mother the vision. Surprised by the sudden change in manners of her son, she gave thanks to the Lord, and amiably congratulated him for such a change. She encouraged him to persevere in the good sentiments he had conceived, and to follow God in the measure His infinite mercy had made known to him. The words of his mother added stimulus to the deep impression that the blessed vision had left in him, and from that moment he purposed to change his life completely.

With fervent tears, Galgano asked God to forgive the foul deeds he had committed, and he suddenly understood all the ingratitude of which he had been guilty towards the Creator and the Redeemer of mankind.

All the earthly delights, entertainment, and pomps being left behind, he retired to his father's house, and for some years, it is believed for 4 or 5, led an obscure and penitent life.

THE TRUE STORY OF THE SWORD IN THE STONE

CHAPTER III
He is Admonished in a Vision to Retire to Mount Siepi[1] to do Penance.

The Lord looked with favor on the change and perseverance of Galgano, in whom such grace had been worked, and He deigned to send another vision in order that He might call him to a very great penance, one to which Galgano was destined by Divine mercy.

Once more, while Galgano slept, St. Michael the Archangel appeared to him. With mysterious images, the Archangel made known that he ought to embark on the path to Mount Siepi, about four miles distant from Chiusdino. At that time, it was a solitary place covered in thick forest. There he

---

[1] Siepi, in Italian means "hurdles" or "obstacles to overcome." -Translator's note.

must offer up every worldly comfort as a sacrifice for his past sins and carry out the most bitter penances.

Galgano was anxious to tell his mother the new vision. Sadly, she who had so desired the conversion of her son, as well as his return to sober and good conduct, also longed so very much to have him close so that he might bring relief to her advanced age and that he might stabilize the succession of the family. Thus, she was greatly disturbed at the thought of losing him, and tried to persuade him that he could still serve God in society, that he should not abandon her once more when she was in necessity, and while he undertook good behavior, she needed much consolation.

Grace had already taken possession of his heart, and began to lift it above all human respect, so that all things should yield to the Divine will. It is best for a man that he ought to come to what has been prescribed by God, to Whom we owe everything, and without Whom we would be nothing, for His commands are sacrosanct, and a man can not transgress them without impiety. Galgano pleaded with prayers and tears, but it so displeased Dionisia to be deprived of her son again, that he did not attempt other means of

THE TRUE STORY OF THE SWORD IN THE STONE

trying it. Not satisfied, she turned to her relatives and took counsel with them. Together they determined that they should propose a girl to Galgano as a spouse ... such a one that he could not refuse.

CHAPTER IV
Galgano's Relatives Come to Propose him a Bride, and he sets off to see Her.

here was at *Civitella* (a big castle about 20 miles distant from Chiusdino on that side of the Maremma), a man by the name of Antonio Brizzi. Fortune had made him very wealthy though he was of common birth. He had a daughter by the name of Polissena, who was very beautiful and charming. Galgano's mother set her heart upon the idea of marrying Polissena to her son, as did his other relatives, and they sought out Brizzi to pursue their purpose. Having made an agreement as to the marriage contract, they proposed it to Galgano. Though he resisted every argument and persuasion for a long time, eventually he was won over by their persistence, and he forgot, for a moment, the injunction received from the Archangel. Thus, he promised

THE TRUE STORY OF THE SWORD IN THE STONE

to go to see the lady Polissena.

With this purpose in mind, Galgano quickly prepared to make the journey from Chiusdino heading towards Civitella. He had not yet gone four miles, when suddenly, in the plain called Morella (near Luriano), his horse stopped and refused to move one step further, though spurred and struck with much energy. Galgano dismounted, and fell down upon his knees. He immediately recognized his failure, and implored forgiveness and help from the Lord so fervently that he saw again the Archangel St. Michael, no longer merely in a vision, but in reality. Right away he gave the command that Galgano should follow him to Mount Siepi. The Archangel then left, saying that there on Mount Siepi Galgano must do harsh penance, being as of that very moment enrolled in the army of heaven.

Overwhelmed and contrite Galgano fell to the ground, and, having drawn his sword from his side he exclaimed, "How you deign, O merciful Lord to show so much favor to a miserable sinner! Ah, but I could more easily plunge my sword into this stone, than obtain forgiveness for my many sins." Having said this, he thrust his sword into the rock, until the whole of it was immersed up to the hilt. This may be observed even in our times

THE TRUE STORY OF THE SWORD IN THE STONE

[2014], in the present Chapel of S. Galgano above Mount Siepi, where there is a boulder with the sword enveloped in stone and guarded well by an iron grate.

In view of this singular miracle, every fear as well as every importune care was banished from Galgano's mind, and he began to back away reverently, fervently venerating the cruciform shape that the sword's hilt now presented to him, as it was now swallowed by rock up to the hilt. Galgano wished to observe nothing else, that he might have continually before his eyes the infinite mercy of the Lord.

The sword of St. Galgano, as it can still be seen today in Galgano, Italy, near Siena.

CHAPTER V
The Beginning of his Penance.

t would be difficult—and indeed it is not allowed for me to describe—the contemplative and penitential life which Galgano led for the space of a year, less two days, wherein he remained until his holy death. Yet, what was received by God we do know, for the graces dispensed by his intercession produced the swift and constant devotion in the hearts of the people inspired by Heaven towards our saint. There were many other signs of Divine favor as well, but this is neither the time nor the place to go into them just now. The brevity of his penance should not surprise us, since the Lord, Who granted equal wages to the workers that came to work in the vineyard at the last hour of the day, as to those who went early in the morning, and Who showed us the piety of the father of the

prodigal son that a true repentance, a firm hope and a burning love disarm promptly all its penalties. That God knew how sincere were the first tears of Mary Magdalene, and sent her back affectionately justified; He is the only just appraiser of our merits, only searcher of hearts, only exact distributor of thanks; and we have to adore His infinite justice and mercy, and thank Him for what He has so freely imparted without our own merit, while recognizing that it is only through one's own fault if one fails to bear interest for those talents that each individual has received.

Galgano increasingly became more fervent in the rigor of his penance, both in fasting, which the locality forced since no food could be found other than roots and some wild fruit, as well as in the rigor of the climate (since he began to make his home there on December 1 without any shelter). He suffered the instant deprivation of any comfort and all pleasure, as well as all human company. These were no small sufferings for Galgano, since need afflicts the flesh very much, and until then he had lived in the very midst of comfort and solace.

The evil seducer thought the disgust of such a harsh life could encourage his evil designs, so

The True Story of the Sword in the Stone

he set about removing Galgano from this place by making the comforts and the friends he had left behind appear temptingly in his imagination. At other times he brought to Galgano's mind the difficulty of continuing among so many deprivations, striving sometimes to scare him with various terrors, which increased the loneliness and sadness of the place. It was always in vain because the grace of the Lord preserved him in every encounter. Once God comforted him with a lovely miracle of four oaks bending over him, weaving their branches together to shelter him far more comfortably than the shack he had made for himself. Thus God willed for Galgano to remain in order to confound and destroy the evil adversary.

Seeing that he could not win in this way, the enemy of mankind began instead to attack Galgano's conscience with respect to money and goods that he may have appropriated unjustly during his earlier life. The evil one made it seem to Galgano that it would be a good thing to go back to Chiusdino and work at acquiring the needed goods to return everything out of justice. Having anything left, he could remain and distribute it amongst the poor. It seemed likely, to the devil, that having once again returned to civilization, Galgano would be loathe to return to his penitential life.

Since Galgano had already abandoned all cares, and had firm trust in God, he was waiting for the means therewith to accomplish this restitution without leaving the place of his retirement. With the grace of God he avoided this new and most alluring deception, dressed up in the most honest of appearances, and he remained waiting for the right moment with firm faith that the propitious moment would arrive in short order.

THE TRUE STORY OF THE SWORD IN THE STONE

CHAPTER VI
Galgano is Found by Some Hunters that give news of him in Chiusdino; his Mother and Relatives visit him, and also bring the would be Bride.

Some young men of Chiusdino were stringing their bows to hunt in the vicinity of Mount Siepi. One of them went away from his companions and climbed to the summit where he found Galgano. At first the youth could not recognize him, since he was in tattered clothes, his face emaciated, and he was in fervent prayer ... the disruption had not distracted him. Galgano seemed an unknown and extraordinary object. The young man did not know what to think until he looked more closely and recognized this apparition as Galgano. Calling him by name, he said, "What are you doing here in this place? Your mother and everyone else believe you are in Civitella near your bride; now why are you in this wilderness?" To which Galgano replied: "The

The True Story of the Sword in the Stone

Lord called me to this very place, so I should be far from the nonsense of the world. Yet I beg you, for your charity, if you would deign to give me a bit of clothing, in order to repair for the season, as well as for decency." Surprised and moved, the hunter gave him a pelt with which to cover himself, then ran back to Chiusdino to tell everyone he'd found Galgano.

The unexpected news surprised everyone. Some were moved, while others, as unfortunately happens, began to mutter about Galgano by suggesting frivolity and being of unsound mind. After all, how could a man look upon all other human things as despicable when he had formerly put all his trust in them? News came to Galgano's mother, and she came with her relatives who were also taken aback by the news. They wanted to go to him at Mount Siepi so they could try to reason with him and change the young man's mind.

The family worked together as one to try to persuade him to abandon his work and return to Chiusdino. As he was supported by grace, however, he was not only able to resist them and justify his conduct, he was also able to console his mother. But they were not given to defeat! Withdrawing from him, they thought it a good

The True Story of the Sword in the Stone

idea to fetch the proposed bride and her father, Antonio Brizzi, so as not to leave anything untried.

This purpose being achieved, they returned all together to Galgano to try this new and more vigorous assault. The vain maiden, in a lowly act, blushing and sorrowful, nearly reproached him for his disregard. Imagine this spectacle: her father confused, the urgent relatives speaking of going back, and, above all, his mother, sighing and weeping. Together they caused such a scene that, for one to resist, a force was required that was more than human.

Galgano's heart wasn't insensible toward these sweet sentiments, but the Divine remained present, and worldly feelings were already in this respect so revolting that he did not diminish from his purpose. Rather, he resolved to renounce all things forthwith for the love of God, not intent upon mere human satisfaction, but to pursue the true good of souls. Galgano showed his mother that true happiness for them both was to be perfectly conformed to the Divine will in which alone all goods can be found. He spoke to his would be bride so efficaciously, that she was soon made to understand the vanity of worldly satisfaction, and her soul was instantly turned to

THE TRUE STORY OF THE SWORD IN THE STONE

the Lord alone. That very day she attempted to retire to the convent of St. Prospero of Siena, of the Cistercian order, which had just been founded. Indeed, she has been regarded by many as having been the founder of that convent, where she was consecrated to its faculty and there lead an exemplary life.

Next, Galgano spoke to his relatives, and he so ardently convinced them that, silent and thoughtful, they left him, and no more had the courage to disturb him again. Before they left him, he wished for his mother to bless him, commending himself to her prayers, as he did also for all the others, who then narrated in Chiusdino with edification what they had seen and heard.

THE TRUE STORY OF THE SWORD IN THE STONE

CHAPTER VII
Galgano has the Divine approval to receive an Indulgence in Rome.

After surviving this most vigorous temptation, that of blood and friendship, our hermit found peace, and only thought to double his penance and bind himself to Heaven with a more fervent spirit. He conveyed his intention to his mother that, having kept what was necessary to his honest sustenance, he ought to arrange his abiding faculties in favor of the poor, first of all, to any whom he might have damaged in any manner. Then he decided to head to Rome to take indulgences, when it was in the pleasure of the Lord. For several days he prayed for this particular intention. Afterward, having attained with certainty the signs of the Lord's consent, he

The True Story of the Sword in the Stone

disposed himself to the pilgrimage. He suffered and practiced on the road every act of Christian humility, asked for alms and charity, and employed himself in the service of every need he met on his journey. Arriving in Rome, he immediately went to St. Peter's, and there at the foot of a confessor he exposed his past life with such feelings and compunction that it was agreed he ought to receive absolution. It was a confirmation of the forgiveness the merciful God had already manifested through the earlier miracle, when he saw the harshness of the living rock yield to his sword, into which it was wholly submerged.

He visited the seven churches for the acquisition of indulgences then presented himself to Pope Alexander III (of the Bandinelli family of Siena). Galgano was received lovingly, as he was already known to the pontiff by his reputation, and encouraged to ask for whatever he wanted. Galgano replied that he longed for three favors. The first, that His Holiness would continue to persevere in the good governance of the Church. Secondly, he wished that the pope would grant him the relics of the holy martyrs Fabian and Sebastian, as well as Pope Saint Stephen, which he had as his particular patrons. Thirdly,

The True Story of the Sword in the Stone

indulgences for the dead of his family, particularly for his father as well as those still living and, above all, for his mother. The pope replied with this kindly summation, that in the first place he hoped, with the Lord's help, that he would persevere on the path he had undertaken. As to the second, he had given the order that the requested relics should be prepared, and to the third agreed with the usual formalities of the time.[2]

Meanwhile, the rector of Chiusdino, as well as the abbot of an Abbey called Serena (a mile away from there), incited by an infernal spirit, took counsel to assail Galgano in his solitude, to sacrifice him to their envy and impious anger kindled only by his penances which greatly

---

[2] The first request of the Saint is altogether remarkable, and especially in our times would be regarded as risky; but the goodness with which he was heard by the Pope, and the apostolic zeal which the place dictated, honored the applicant and the request. [The foregoing note of the author reflects the times in which this book was written, namely the 1830s. At that time, the Pope was under attack from organized freemasonry (the *Carbonari*) and progressive secular opinion. Thus, such a statement would have been regarded as a criticism of the Pope.
-Translator's note.]

The True Story of the Sword in the Stone

contrasted with their relaxed way of life.

They took with them an armed lay brother to Mount Siepi. Not finding Galgano there, they raged against the sword. Since they could not pluck it up from the rock, they beat it with several blows, breaking it into three pieces which they then threw to the ground. They burned the oaks which formed the hut of the Saint, and destroyed what was there for his use. They then left, but it wasn't long before they were made to pay the penalty of their crimes. On the return journey a horrible storm arose and lightning struck the abbot, the parish priest was drowned in a creek called Righineto, and the lay brother had his arms ripped off by two wild wolves. By Divine permission, as a reminder of this occurrence, these same arms are still preserved intact in the chapel mentioned above.

THE TRUE STORY OF THE SWORD IN THE STONE

CHAPTER VIII
Galgano has a Revelation of what happened while in Rome, urges the Pope for the Relics, and Returns to Mount Siepi

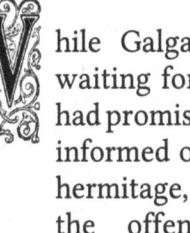hile Galgano was staying in Rome waiting for the relics, which the pope had promised him, he was miraculously informed of what had happened to his hermitage, as well as what had befallen the offenders. Their demise he lamented more than any injuries he had received from them. Intent upon returning to his solitude, he urged from the pope the promised relics. When questioned by the pontiff about several things, he related that he was informed by an angel of the damage done to the sword hilt which served as his cross, the ruination of his hut, and the exemplary punishment of the evil-doers. The pope, astonished and fearing it to be true as he claimed, sent with the utmost care and secrecy a

THE TRUE STORY OF THE SWORD IN THE STONE

quick messenger to Mount Siepi, and ordered Galgano to come back to him in a few days. The saint obeyed, and prayed to Heaven that the mind of the pope should be moved to let him go.

He went back at the predetermined time, and found the pope to be in a better disposition, having been inspired by the Lord that he should no longer delay his servant. Therefore he would send him, and handed over the relics to him. At this moment the messenger returned, bringing the most exact confirmation of what Galgano had related. The pope was surprised and moved. Therefore he blessed him, and recommended himself to the saint's prayers, since he had already discerned in him a true servant of God.

With the precious treasures he so desired, Galgano departed from Rome and resumed his pilgrimage on the road to his hermitage. The distance of time, lack of memory, and above all, the saint's humility led him entirely to ignore the many acts of Christian virtue he exercised on that arduous journey, as well as the many graces he received from the Lord.

Finally he came to Mount Siepi, and upon seeing the havoc committed by those wicked men, he became so sorrowful and disheartened that he thought he should choose another place

The True Story of the Sword in the Stone

more segregated and far away. There, quietly and without fear of any disturbance, he could abandon himself in all the fervor of his penances. But Heaven prodigiously made him resolve that he ought to remain there. He began to take into his hand the pieces of the broken sword, and prayed to the Lord that He would will to grant him to venerate the hilt in the image of the cross as he had done before his departure, and drawing them together, prayed they might be miraculously united. Heaven granted his request, and upon having witnessed another miracle from on high, Galgano burst into thanksgiving and tender effusions of his heart towards his Benefactor and loving Father. He placed the sword remade into the same opening that was first formed so miraculously.

THE TRUE STORY OF THE SWORD IN THE STONE

CHAPTER IX
The Penitential Life of Galgano and some Graces Obtained through his Intercession.

After fervent prayers Galgano thought to build a hut of planks, since it was not possible to be exposed to the winter elements without coming down with a serious disease. It was of such small dimension so as to be just tight enough to cover him, requiring little labor to build. Being so settled, he ordered his daily occupations, employing those few hours in which he desisted from prayer to cut wood and make bundles of kindling in service of the poor. These he took to the public road, where he made a ditch for them so they could be collected by the poor without fatigue, to free them from the loss of time they suffered when they were previously

THE TRUE STORY OF THE SWORD IN THE STONE

obliged to find them in the woods.[3]

He learned, meanwhile, of a holy man named William, who had assembled a community of religious penitents in common life about 25 miles from him, where there were to be seen wonderful fruits of the spiritual life. The desire was enkindled in him to participate in some fashion in such goods, and if he could not go there continuously, at least from time to time he might go to join the prayers of this community.

This being carried into effect, he obtained enrollment in their institution without taking away from his hermit's life. As often as he could he went there to contribute to the common prayers and be refreshed with the Bread of Angels.

Soon renown of the examplary life of Galgano spread and waves of heavenly favors bore fruit. So many signs clearly appeared that crowds of

---

[3] Today this might seem as a minor work. However, in the 12th century, peasants spent a great deal of time collecting firewood for their heat, laundry, and kitchen. We can understand what a great act of charity this is when we realize that whole days were saved for women and children to spend more time with their families or in prayer rather than in collecting firewood. -Translator's note.

people were moved to build their homes in sight of the holy man so as to have counsel, that he might intercede for them with the Lord. This was not in vain, since he in turn attended to various lame as well as those afflicted with various infirmities, who were then returned to their former health, in body and in soul. He humbled them with grave admonitions and exhortations to fully change their ways, as is more fully said in the history of Father Lombardelli, and as we have it in the office of the saint. Here are the exact words: "Desiring to hide from renown, gleaming with holy virtues, renown nevertheless spread throughout Tuscany; women soon came from parts of Arrezo with great faith. Blessed Galgano obtained gifts of graces to the devoted faithful of Christ and all those coming to him."[4] Elsewhere: "Being filled with great virtue, Blessed Galgano destroyed vices, put demons to flight, cured the sick, ordered morals, informed virtues, and

---

[4]

Fama latere cupiens, sanctis micans virtutibus, diffunditur in Thuscia; mulieres mox venere de Aretii partibus cum maxima fiducia. Dona gratiarum beatus Galganus obtinet devotis Christi fidelibus ad se venientibus.

merited all this from the grace of holiness;"[5] and, as it is stated elsewhere in the office: "The lame, lepers, sick, captives and weak whom apathy had long wearied out, the physician of heaven had restored to health through Christ."[6]

---

[5] Virtute manga beatus Galganus perimit vitia, fugat daemones, curat languores, mores ordinat, informat virtutes, et hoc promeruit ex gratia sanctitatis.

[6] Claudos, leprosos, languidos, captivos, et invalidos quos longus languor enuit, ad pristinum restituit per ipsum coeli medicus.

THE TRUE STORY OF THE SWORD IN THE STONE

CHAPTER X
The Death of St. Galgano

St. Galgano continued his strict abstinence, penance and the harsh life that he practiced. His ailing body, formerly addicted to so many pleasures and comforts, was rendered completely indisposed by them. So ill was he that, on the feast day of St. Andrew (the last day of November in the year of our Savior, 1181) he was attacked by so violent a fever, originating in his chest, that it carried him away within three days. Away his soul flew to live eternally in the Bosom of the Lord.

His precious death happened on the third day of December, in his 33rd year of age, after a year of retirement, for he had ascended to Mount Siepi on December 1 of the year before, 1180. Though hidden from the eyes of men, for it is to be

The True Story of the Sword in the Stone

supposed that in that rough season not as many of the faithful were frequently brought to visit him, God wanted to make wonderfully manifest the glorification of His servant and procure for him those earthly honors, that, when they are bestowed unto blessed happiness, they are to honor the Lord in His elect very directly. For example, He provided for the decent burial of the martyr Catherine, as well as Paul the First Hermit, Anthony and Mary of Egypt, and also for our Galgano. Without a miracle from his provident care, they would have long remained unburied and exposed to the ravages of wild beasts, as well as the seasons.

THE TRUE STORY OF THE SWORD IN THE STONE

CHAPTER XI
God Miraculously Provides for his Burial.

In the Serena Valley, the bishop of Massa Marittima (of whom nothing is known except his name) and the bishop of Volterra Hugh of Saladini (a nobleman of the Count d'Agnano), whose sacred memory is venerated, met on the day of the transitus of Galgano.

Questioning each other on the object of their journey, the bishop of Massa said that he went to Siena for some business. The bishop of Volterra remarked that he was brought from his diocese to Chiusdino because there was a present need to provide for the replacement of the priest, the latter person and the abbot of the Serena Valley having perished so miserably in an unjust aggression made on Mount Siepi (as was related above). All of this, he told to the bishop of Massa. It was his intention to visit the hermit Galgano

THE TRUE STORY OF THE SWORD IN THE STONE

after his business was completed. The same desire was enkindled in the bishop of Massa.

Suspending the trip to Chiusdino, he wished to be brought immediately to Galgano. They turned, making their way while thinking on the road of his wonderful penances, as well as the graces of one so favored by the Lord. At the summit of the mountain, approaching the hut, they saw him kneeling down on the other side. Supposing him to be in deep contemplation they stood back a pace so as not to disturb him, but waited in such a way that naturally would cause him to turn. To that end, they made a little noise, but seeing that he was still motionless and in the same posture, they entered the hut and approached him, only to discover that he had passed from this life.

They felt deep pain for not having arrived at least a few hours earlier that they might have assisted him in his last moments, and to hear from his holy mouth words of consolation and edification, since it was this most ardent desire which had driven them there. They mourned that they had missed a living mirror of contrition, penance and spiritual vitality, but consoled themselves with the thought that they would in some way be compensated by giving the holy

The True Story of the Sword in the Stone

hermit the honors of burial.

While the bishops had sent a few of their servants to seek people in order to accomplish this pious ceremony, three abbots appeared on the Mount with various monks of the Cistercian order returning into Italy from the general chapter of their rule held in France. Owing to the bad weather of the sea, they were constrained to take to the land route of the Sienese Maremma, and became lost on the road. They understood from the rambling of their guides that there was, nearby, a Roman road going in the direction they wished to travel in. Surprised to find two bishops in such a bitter wilderness, they expounded to them the mistake which had happened and asked if they could be provided with a guide. The bishops recognized in the abbots' arrival a decidedly Divine arrangement, and they declared that it was not by chance but by the will of heaven that they had arrived so that they could offer the final duties to the holy man whose life and deeds they briefly narrated.

Meanwhile, news of Galgano's death arrived at Chiusdino, and also to other nearby places surrounding it. This spurred a great mass of people to begin the journey to visit Galgano, his body adorned with the effects of maceration and

The True Story of the Sword in the Stone

fasting, an air of sanctity hovering about, moving everyone to compunction. Some who were sick had themselves dragged up to him in order to obtain through his intercession the recovery of their health. A leper instantly obtained liberation from that disgusting disease; a woman brought her little son, being seriously injured by an accident, and knelt before the saint... instantaneously he was healed! So many other favors were bestowed by the Lord on that occasion that their devotion was increased all the more. All that stood around broke into tears and loudly proclaimed the sanctity of Galgano.

The priests carried out the sacred rites and gave his remains an honorable burial in the same place where the sword was driven into the rock.

THE TRUE STORY OF THE SWORD IN THE STONE

CHAPTER XII
The Origin of the Chapel and Abbey of St. Galgano.

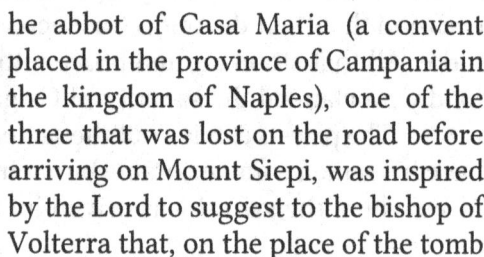he abbot of Casa Maria (a convent placed in the province of Campania in the kingdom of Naples), one of the three that was lost on the road before arriving on Mount Siepi, was inspired by the Lord to suggest to the bishop of Volterra that, on the place of the tomb of the saint, a chapel in his honor should be erected, as well as a house for a few monks to celebrate Mass, which he would provide from his own community. The proposition pleased the bishop, who gave his permission to build, and generous people made large offerings.

In the space of five years the chapel was completed that is, to this day, preserved intact. Of solid and austere construction, it is perfectly

The True Story of the Sword in the Stone

round, over of 29-30 feet in diameter,[7] with a tall dome and lantern, the entire interior of which was painted with the deeds of the saint. Such paintings were perhaps worn out by time and forgotten, leading to uncultivated men covering them with new mortar and whitewashing them... now not even a vestige of them remains, nothing more than one bezel in a small chapel next to the church.

As a result of the people's devotion, it grew dramatically. The graces and miracles worked from heaven through the intercession of Galgano from his tomb served to increase the offers and the gifts of the neighboring cities, both of various prelates and princes, who are to serve as proof of the merits of our saint. There were some ideas to erect a more grandiose church and, in like manner, a larger convent. The location of the mountain did not afford the necessary space, however, but at the foot of the mountain, 66 years after the death of Galgano, an immense and majestic church was built, as well as the Abbey of

---

[7] The measurements are a rough approximation of the braccio legno, or "wooden arm" measurement in use from the middle ages until the late 19th century, and used by the author, which is approximately 1.78 ft. -Translator's note.

THE TRUE STORY OF THE SWORD IN THE STONE

Saint Galgano. It was said that it garnered the admiration of the time, but, due to a series of mournful circumstances, it was left to utterly waste away, as is seen in today. The magnificent ruins, however, are still a subject of amazement.

The ruins extend over the immense shrine and monastery in a quadrangular space of not less than 711 feet on each side. The church is 231 feet long internally over a width of 80 ft in three aisles, and 112 ft in the cross section; the quickness and austere form of its Gothic architecture, the rich marble and stonework, are shining witness of these majestic ruins, which still remain today. The aqueducts are also observed at the present. In their day, they provided excellent and abundant water collected with great effort and expense which have their sources from distant places, so it is little wonder that it maintained itself in prosperous times. From authentic memory more than 180 monks, priests, and a proportionate amount of the laity dwelt there. There were so many homes containing different arts and crafts that it could be said to have formed a city, populated by over 4000 souls and now (alas, the terrible story of human things!) destroyed, desolate and lonely.

It is not the purpose of this compendium to

expose the causes of the decay of time, which must above all else be attributed to pestilence, particularly in the sixteenth century, which exercised its deadly might. Other sources may be consulted in order to have more widespread publicity; the writers of the histories of Siena, Malavolti Pecci, as well as others. One can find a sensible account in the recent *Dizionario geografico, fisico, e storico della Toscana*, which is published by Mr. Emanuelle Repetti in the Article: "*Abazia di San Galgano.*"

I thought to briefly mention something about the magnificence of such a famous shrine, only to make it understood how much the reverence was no less present in the surrounding people that, although from remote places, contributed such a quality of work dedicated to our Saint. Certainly, without having seen the favors which Heaven continually imparted to his intercession, they were not in fact his contemporaries, for the next generation generously accepted the gifts, and bountiful offerings in his honor.

The True Story of the Sword in the Stone

Chapter XIII
Galgano is Canonized and Enrolled in the Number of Confessors, and some Miracles.

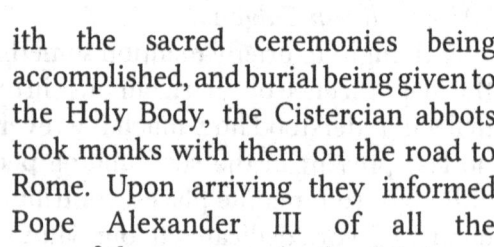ith the sacred ceremonies being accomplished, and burial being given to the Holy Body, the Cistercian abbots took monks with them on the road to Rome. Upon arriving they informed Pope Alexander III of all the circumstances of the precious death of Galgano. Not very long after, a solemn embassy equipped for providing the processes, faith and testimony to his holiness was sent to the same pontiff from the city of Siena, as well as the community of Chiusdino. They brought with them no less than the earnest supplications of many religious and famous people for the canonization of Galgano.

The Supreme Shepherd, who had known the saint in Rome on the occasion of his pilgrimage, recalled to himself the miraculous revelation he

THE TRUE STORY OF THE SWORD IN THE STONE

had (of the destruction of his hermitage and punishment of its destroyers), as well as his outstanding virtue. He found the demand agreeable, and with great care and the consent of the sacred college, along with any other necessary formalities, canonized Galgano and added him to the number of confessors. He also ordered that both the office and the feast were to be carried out on the day of his death, that is, on December 3, so that as a very rare example, he was enrolled in the number of the Saints in less than a year from his death, by the same pontiff who predicted that at the end of the year he would pass to a better life.

In the meantime, many notable miracles were worked at his tomb, some of which are recorded in his office.

A child of 8 years fell into a nearby river and drowned, but was recalled to life: "Reddens vitae puerum demersum in fluvio, solatur patrem miserum suo patrocinio." He freed a woman possessed by the devil for seven years: "Vexatam a daemonio mulierem septinnio, latam oratorio, suo curat suffragio." An innocent man who had been maligned was imprisoned in the Val d'Orcia, but he escaped by flight and was pursued by the jailers. As they were about to overtake him, he was miraculously taken out of their sight: "Clausus Orciae carcere, fugit ab ergastulo, Sanctus Dei munere liberat a periculo."

A woman's broken hand was restored to life: "Visitans Sancti limina, contracta manu foemina, cum sanitatis gratia, laeta redit ad propria."

Many others are more widely reported in the life written by Father Lombardelli, of which I limit myself to a brief compendium.

CHAPTER XIV
Extraction of his Precious Relics, and Especially the Sacred Head.

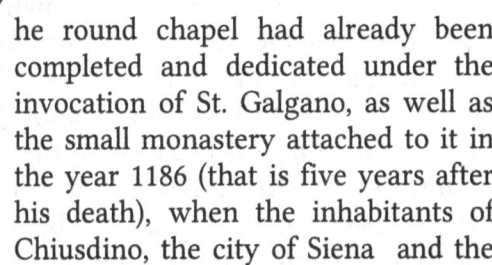he round chapel had already been completed and dedicated under the invocation of St. Galgano, as well as the small monastery attached to it in the year 1186 (that is five years after his death), when the inhabitants of Chiusdino, the city of Siena and the monks simultaneously desired to have some relics of his holy body. It was decided to exhume it. Assistant members, being authorized to undertake this task, excavated and removed the body, and found his head and his face were preserved as they were in life, while the rest of the body was somewhat decayed. The head, after being severed and placed in a special reliquary, was then exposed for public veneration. The rest of his body was laid in a decent casket, back in its place,

THE TRUE STORY OF THE SWORD IN THE STONE

so that later it could be extracted again to form relics. The last remnants were re-interred in a casket of lead sealed on four sides with the inscription: "Ossa S. Galgani." The holy head was placed on the altar of the chapel where it was venerated for a long time, until the Abbey was dispelled, and the church at the foot of the mountain moved so that the functions could be carried out more decorously.

In every sinister event, for every need, the city of Siena and other surrounding towns went to implore the Divine Aid through his intercession, and frequently his relics were carried in procession to Siena in times of famine, pestilence and for obtaining graces expressly implored. As a result, the citizens of Siena wished to keep the relics permanently. To avoid the difficulties inherent with the long trip and the irreverence which could happen to them, it is believed that, around the year 1300, they were placed in the monastery of St. Prosper of Siena near the porta Camollia where Polissena Brizzi, the bride promised to Galgano, was vested as a nun (and later died in the odor of sanctity), as was mentioned above in chapter VI.

There the head remained for a short time, until it was taken to the cathedral in order to

The True Story of the Sword in the Stone

secure it from the hands of devoted kidnappers who had more than once tried to rush upon it. Being at last successful in their plan, they took it with them out of the city, when, between the door and the gate called Camollia, they were lost in the lawn that then existed. Suddenly, as if they were in thick woods, they could not find the exit, until, surprised by supernatural terror, they set down the sacred head on the ground, found the exit with ease and fled. This great miracle is preserved in the memory of the door, where there is, above the arch on the guard's side, a painting depicting the head in a tabernacle that has two angels lifted up off the earth to bring it back to the monastery of St. Prospero, as in fact happened.

Later, the head of St. Galgano was placed in the cathedral, and after that, it was transferred to the Church of the Hospital of La Scala in front of the cathedral in order to satisfy the devotion of the poor patients. In 1477, at the request of the monks of the Abbey of San Galgano, it was taken to their hospice, which was near the bridge in the vicinity of the Porta Romana. It was called "The Magdalene" and the Abbot at the time was named Bartolommeno. On that occasion he compensated the hospice and the church for their inestimable

The True Story of the Sword in the Stone

loss by placing the precious relic at the altar. More recently, in 1550, it was brought to where it rests presently, that is in the church and monastery of St. Mary of the Angels, commonly called the Santuccio next to the Porta Romana.

The many translations were caused by either the fear that the head would be abducted, or the fervent desire of various devotees who longed to possess it, though we do not know for sure in either instance. What we do know, however, is that wherever it was, it was indeed always held in veneration, and conducted frequently in procession through the city in any urgent need.

When Father Lombardelli wrote to say farewell in 1577, it was perfectly preserved and intact, as revealed from his narrative in this regard, where, after having described the magnificence of the reliquary formed of precious metal, enriched with gems and adorned with an engraved legend in outline describing the most remarkable actions of the saint, the following words evince its condition:

> "This most precious head is forthright in all parts; and in front has a small and subtle scratch on the right side. It is beardless, but with full head of hair as

The True Story of the Sword in the Stone

cloth of gold, that has a veneer like silk; it's look is jolly, nearer to being full of bright color that lights up as if it were alive, and with a few freckles: such that in sum I believe few relics can compare with it. I do not possess sufficient ink to write with a pen how beautiful it seems, both concerning the person and the mind, when many years are all seen. But as for the many miracles God has shown it, I will say in the next chapter. "

From this description it is gathered that over the course of four centuries the sacred head had been preserved as though it were alive. Now, below the eyelashes is reduced almost to a skeleton, retaining only a little bit of skin on the cheeks, but the forehead and scalp are always in pristine condition, retaining the hair seen since the time of Father Lombardelli.

The True Story of the Sword in the Stone

Chapter XV
The Veneration in which the Sacred Head is always held, and the Various Miracles Granted to its Intercession.

In sum, during the entire time it was venerated in Siena, so many favors were obtained through the sacred head's intercession (even from the first moment it was transferred from the Abbey of St. Galgano in 1300), that "it was deemed fit to establish that, twice a year, it would be conveyed around the city in order that the public desire to venerate the head could be satisfied. The feasts of Pentecost and the Assumption of Mary were the two most frequently chosen."

In the year 1477, for famine, pestilence and calamity, the rulers of the republic made a record of the many favors obtained through the intercession of the saint. In the city council held

THE TRUE STORY OF THE SWORD IN THE STONE

in the palace of the Signory, marked by a resolution of 28 April, 1477, it was stated that on the 3rd day of December, the commemoration of the saint was to be observed as a public holiday, and that for the two processions spoken of above, the sacred head was to be accompanied by ten different people with torches and the insignia of the Republic, as well as four gentlemen to support the canopy, as is done on the day of St. Rocco.

Simultaneously they transported, accompanied by those ceremonies, the head of St. Catherine the apostolic virgin and the arm of the martyr St. Ansanus, the first promulgator of the Holy Gospel in that city.

The ceremonies surrounding the sacred head of St. Galgano lasted for many years, but with the passing of time most of the usual processions were left out for various reasons. The head is not taken out now except from time to time for Low Sunday[8], the custom on that day being to make the procession with some of the various images

---

[8] Low Sunday, in Latin *Dominica in Albis*, was from time immemorial the term for the Sunday immediately after Easter, until the reform of the Calendar following Vatican II, whereas now it is known as *Divine Mercy Sunday* since the pontificate of Pope Saint John Paul II. -Translator's note.

THE TRUE STORY OF THE SWORD IN THE STONE

and relics that are useful in greater devotions, and by now it has been more than 40 years since it has been taken out for various reasons.

In the same year, 1477, the University of Siena (called *della Seta*), chose Saint Galgano in particular as its Patron. Many are the miracles that brought attention to the sacred head at all times, as the ancient chronicles and traditions reveal, and many of those reports in this regard Fr. Lombardelli considered more authentic. From these I will choose some.

At the time that it was brought back from Siena to the Abbey of San Galgano, a troop willing to kidnap it was placed in ambush on the road; when the lead mare, upon which the head had been placed, came near to them it began to double its pace of its own will, until it could not in any way be reached. The danger passed, they brought the head to the doors of the chapel where the body was, lest anyone should wish to remove it. As soon as they reached those who were chosen for the guardianship of the head, they easily guided it to the Abbey's care.

On another occasion all storms appeared to have ceased, and the sky became instantly clear.

During some of the festivals, when the head was exposed for public veneration, it seemed to exude a fragrant liquor that brought health to the sick when they were recommended with lively faith to the Lord through the intercession of the saint.

The hair has been cut many times for relics and has always returned to pristine length, a miracle which continues to this day. It is always preserved very long and abundant, though often it has been cut to the end, and again recently, I myself have seen it with my own eyes in same quantity and length as it is described by Father Lombardelli, and everyone who is led to venerate the sacred head can attest to this.

The True Story of the Sword in the Stone

Conclusion

Here is a brief compendium of what, at length, is treated in the often cited history to which I hope to have been faithful, now taking great care to speak about some wonderful visions that occurred in places where the saint lived and did penance, which were received in that place at the end of the year 1831, 1832 and in 1833, in the person of two young maids whom I questioned myself many times, and carefully examined.

As to others who received visions, still I found them even more conformed and constant; their very words are consistent in the spirit of these people, the living proof of the genuineness and of the truth of what they have claimed. There is no doubt of the excitement and the spiritual fruit that has grown in this circumstance. The improvement of morals and the growth of an

The True Story of the Sword in the Stone

extremely religious spirit are unconscious arguments of grace that beareth fruit in souls through the Divine seed. But even more the church has not yet recognized, and I am silently and impatiently waiting for this new favor.

Meanwhile, availing myself of God's mercy, I hope to imitate the penitent saint's life, though unfortunately I have not become exceedingly advanced, wherefore I might attain that only good for which we were created and to which every true heart desires.

Finis

THE TRUE STORY OF THE SWORD IN THE STONE

EPILOGUE
by dom Noah Moerbeek,
Christi Pauperum Militiae Templi Ordo

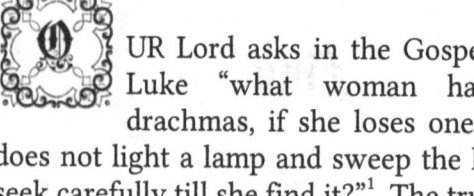UR Lord asks in the Gospel of Saint Luke "what woman having ten drachmas, if she loses one drachma, does not light a lamp and sweep the house and seek carefully till she find it?"[1] The true story of the sword and the stone, and the marvelous conversion of St. Galgano, is one of those coins that we hope with this little work will light a lamp to the cave of conversion, where a sword became a cross.

The lives of many popular saints today have become as so many coins to enrich the hearts of the faithful: St. Thérèse for her Little Way, St. Padre Pio for his obedience and suffering, St.

---

[1] Luke 15:8.

The True Story of the Sword in the Stone

Louis De Monforte for his Total Consecration to Mary, and so on. But, what in the life of St. Galgano, a knight and a hermit, can enrich the faithful today?

I found out about St. Galgano when I became a novice in the Militia Templi[2] as he was a Patron of our Order. I was taught that he was a Knight, and was given a very brief account of the sword and the stone. I also received a prayer card with his collect and picture on it, blessed with a first class relic of him, when I went through the ritual to become a Novice at Christ in the Desert Monastery in New Mexico[3].

---

[2] Under the jurisdiction of the Catholic Archdiocese of Siena, the Militia Templi's members follow a modern adaptation of the Rule written by St. Bernard of Clairvaux for the Templars.

[3] The Cardinal Protectors of the Militia Templi were Silvio Oddi, Édouard Gagnon and Alfons Maria Stickler. The current Protector is Phillip Lawrence, OSB, Abbot of the Benedictine Monastery of Christ in the Desert New Mexico, USA.

The True Story of the Sword in the Stone

Our rule and constitutions[4] are designed primarily with the idea of a community of brothers praying and working together; however, in the United States, the Knights are relatively isolated and live at great distances from one another. Without the help and consolations of community life we have often recalled the example of St. Galgano to encourage one another.

Catholics today who wish to fully live their faith often find themselves isolated in their local Church and even in their own family. St. Galgano's mother prayed for his conversion, but despite her piety, became an obstacle to his vocation when he became a hermit.

Was God's will for Galgano to become a missionary? To start a new devotion or write down spiritual visions? Perhaps, become a great teacher? No. God called Galgano to adore the sign of his salvation, the Holy Cross.

God performed a miracle to show how easy it is to forgive our sins, and St. Galgano embraced a life of penance. Today, it seems very few Christians doubt the mercy and love of God, but

---

[4] The constitutions were approved on Sept. 8, 1988, by the Archbishop of Siena Mario Jsmaele. Castellano. Archbishop Gaetano Bonicelli approved the Rule of the Militia in 1990.

THE TRUE STORY OF THE SWORD IN THE STONE

are there great fruits of repentance? Our Blessed Lord said, "unless you shall do penance, you shall all likewise perish"[5] while today it would seem that some live and teach that to do real penance is to somehow foster a doubt that God has forgiven us. Blessed Columba Marmion said that penance is the "greatest possible assurance of perseverance in the way of perfection – because it is, when one really looks at it, one of the purest forms of love."[6]

St. Galgano faced the hardships of nature, the persecution of family and temptations from the devil to separate him from the sign of his salvation. This penitential life was too much for some. Even the local abbot and priest set out to harm him because of the rebuke that such steadfastness offered to their laxity.

The assault on sanctuaries, devotions, piety and the malicious assaults on the faithful are all the more common in our time. The wicked clerics were successful in molesting his hermitage, but "The Lord keepeth all them that love Him; but all the wicked He will destroy."[7] Galgano's sword that was broken by their malice

---

[5] Luke 13:3.
[6] Christ, the Life of the Soul; Bk. 2 Ch. 4.
[7] Psalm 145:20.

THE TRUE STORY OF THE SWORD IN THE STONE

was restored through Galgano's prayer. We can be assured that God will not allow the cross to be taken from us and the wicked who seek to destroy these things will themselves be destroyed.

Do we live lives of sin, indulgence and comfort, full of too much free time? So did St. Galgano. Perhaps we gave up a life of heavy sin to embrace a more devout life, but lapsed in our devotion at some point. So did St. Galgano. Despite these two things, St. Galgano came to great sanctity, from the moment the sword entered the stone, to his death one year later. If God numbers all things,[8] and Galgano had resisted God's last call with but one year to live, he would have died before he had ever enjoyed a long marriage and would have never become the great Saint that he is.

We know not how much time we have left, and if we examine ourselves, will we find that we have done any worthy penance for our sins? If we cooperate with God to make us into great Saints, He can do so in a short amount of time, as He did with St. Galgano.

May God, through the intercession of St Galgano, drive the sword of His Gospel through our hard hearts, that we might fully embrace the

---

[8] Wisdom 11:21.

The True Story of the Sword in the Stone

Holy Cross and become rooted in penance sprung out of faith in Christ, hope in salvation, and the love of the Crucified Jesus.

Saint Galgano, pray for us.

www.ingramcontent.com/pod-product-compliance
Lightning Source LLC
Chambersburg PA
CBHW011131070526
44583CB00023B/2992